OVERCOMING TOXICITY IN MARRIAGE

How to build a glorious home

Yemi Adebanjo

I dedicate this book to my spiritual parents; Pastor Gabriel and Mrs. Comfort Ogundipe, who clocked 40 years of marriage on April 24, 2022, I pray for more abundant grace and love over your family in Jesus' name.

CONTENTS

Title Page

Copyright

Dedication

Foreword

Introduction

Acknowledgement

God's Original Plan for Marriage   1

The Devil's Plan   5

Devil and The First Home   10

The Forbidden Fruit   15

Separated to be Eliminated   19

Conflict Management   22

Conflict First Aid   29

When To Allow The Third Party   35

When Marriage is Life-threatening   39

Divorce and Separation   47

Conclusion   53

About The Author   55

FOREWORD

I am happy to recommend this book because it is inspired by God and because it is also a helpful resource for couples who are looking for a way to strengthen their relationships as husband and wife.

The author, Opeyemi Adebanjo, who is a beloved brother in Christ and a fellow Ambassador of God's Kingdom, has shown that couples can experience heaven on earth in their marriages. With the turn of every page in this book, I found myself praying for my own marriage and the marriages of people who are dear to me. Despite being married for over 10 years, there were lessons in this book for me that cannot be ignored. This book not only provides more insight into marriage but also encourages spouses to take a deeper look at themselves in order to promote healthy relationships as they stand together on God's word to reinforce His purpose for marriage and also defeat the devil. Many couples have a hard time resolving conflicts in their marriages and they soon become constant, thereby leading to a toxic marital relationship. This book exposes the strategy of the devil against homes. The author has carefully addressed the top areas of conflict between married couples.

I recommend this book for intending couples, married couples, churches, schools, and everyone who desires to experience a home that is built on a foundation that can never be shaken by storms. This book offers hope to anyone who might have lost hope in the godly institution. It also reminds every married couple that the battle is against the devil, and so, it is necessary to stand together and be on the Lord's side.

Pastor Mrs. Moronke Oladimeji
Insight Bible Church,
Lekki, Lagos, Nigeria

INTRODUCTION

When I was single and unsure who to marry, I fantasized about having a happy, godly, and beautiful home. This was the mindset I took into my marriage. Checking out the journey of five years of marriage has taught me a lot of things. Despite my preparedness and determination, I still have days when I go against my plan; I still have days when I got angry unexpectedly; I still have days when I made my wife unhappy; but I planned for a home without a fight. What has happened to me that I cannot stand by my plan? Does it mean I have backslid? Does it mean I no longer love my wife?

I want you to know that marriage is broad, and it does not matter how well you prepare; you are coming to learn afresh, and you must be ready to be broken to learn, and that is the secret of a godly marriage. It is unfortunate that the will to fight for a home is fading on a daily basis. Many of our young people are marrying, and their marriage vows are based on for better, not for worse; for richer, not for poorer; and in health, not in sickness. ess. They no longer want a marriage of pain; they no longer want a poor marriage. Nobody planned it; nobody planned for barrenness in marriage; nobody planned for poverty in marriage; it came, and you just have to fight through it.

God's plan for the home is for it to be heaven on earth. We can make it work; a toxic home is not God's plan. Don't give room to the devil to deceive you and ruin your home; don't give room to any friend to talk you out of marriage; whatever happens in your marriage is your plan, and you can change it when you are ready for it.

Things written here were inspired by the Holy Spirit. When I checked what was happening among couples today, I lost my peace, and this message came. I will appeal to you to take enough time to pray. Don't just read; please pray. Be ready to learn and unlearn; be ready to submit to the yoke of discipline. Lamentation 3:27. Allow God to work in you and through you; don't forget that the common enemy you have is the devil. I see God helping your home in Jesus' name.

ACKNOWLEDGEMENT

This book can't be completed without appreciating those whom God has used for me in one way or another.

I want to say thank you to my beloved wife for the peace I am enjoying in my home and for taking time to take care of our children, Princess and Bright, whenever I get busy writing. I appreciate her taking time to proofread this book for me.

I want to say thank you to Pastor Gbenga Adeniyi, pastor-in-charge of Christ Apostolic Church (CAC) Sunti, Niger State, for proofreading the manuscript. My appreciation goes to Pastor Mrs Moronke Oladimeji for proofreading and writing the foreword of this book. I cannot end without saying thank you to Mrs Oluwabunmi Bamitale for taking time to edit this book; your reward is great, ma'am.

Finally, I thank God for making this project a success. I say may His name be praised forever, in Jesus' name.

GOD'S ORIGINAL PLAN FOR MARRIAGE

Chapter One

We must first explore the origin of marriage as much as our focus is on toxic marriage; this will help us understand why fighting for homes is so crucial. Nobody plans for a broken home, especially Christians, yet we now have a lot of Christian single mothers whose husbands have abandoned them or left the marriage due to physical and emotional abuse.

God has been interested in marriage since the beginning of time, which is why He began a marriage plan after creation.

Genesis 2:1-2, Thus the heavens and the earth were finished, and all the host of them. [2] And on the seventh day God ended his work which he had made, and he rested on the seventh day from all his work which he had made.

God rested before the plan for marriage started. To confirm this again, you will see that God made Adam have a sound sleep in

Genesis 2:[21] And the Lord God caused a deep sleep to fall upon Adam, and he slept: and He took one of his ribs, and closed up the flesh instead thereof;

Why will God rest before implementing the plan for marriage, and why will He make the man sleep before removing the bone? Because the Lord has ordained that the force of the husband and wife will command complete rest, I'm not saying there won't be difficulties, but according to the Bible, two forces working together will pursue ten thousand. The Lord has confidence in marriage to the extent that he created the woman from a refined being rather than from the ground. The sand was gathered to create man, and after the man was refined, the woman was called out, because she represents beauty, distinction, and honour, and when she joins these qualities with the man, they will have complete rest from struggle.

See the scripture again, Genesis 1:18 And the Lord God said, It is not good that the man should be alone; I will make him a help meet for him. We could derive two points here; every animal was made both male and female but when it comes to humans, only man was made, second point is that the entity that God want to make is coming as helpmeet for a man, it will be good for us to consider other versions of the scripture here, please let us check it together:
Then the LORD God said, "It's not good that the human is alone. I will make him a helper that is perfect for him." (CEB)
ADONAI, God, said, "It isn't good that the person should be alone. I will make for him a companion suitable for helping him." (CJB)
And the Lord God said, "*It is* not good that man should be alone; I will make him a helper comparable to him." (NKJV)

Looking at the scripture above, it is clear that woman came into the life of man to take the role of a helper. The woman is not a stranger; she is in man, she is of man, she was brought out of man, and that is why when man saw the woman, despite not knowing when the operation was conducted, he said: Genesis 2:23 [23] And Adam said, This is now bone of my bones, and flesh of my flesh: she shall be called Woman because she was taken out of Man. Adam taught us through his narration that she is his bone, his flesh, and that when Eve stands, it is Adam; when Eve makes a decision, it is Adam; and that whatever the woman does, she is standing for the man, and vice versa. Many homes have failed to grasp this concept, which is why we have toxic marriages today. When the revelation has dawn on a man that the woman was taken from him, he will stop beating her or abusing her emotionally.

See again another reflection of God's plan for home as recorded in Isaiah 8:[18] Behold, I and the children whom the Lord hath given me are for signs and for wonders in Israel from the Lord of hosts, which dwelleth in mount Zion. This passage illustrates God's original purpose, in which He formed parents into signs and instructed children to be wonders, for what reason? Because we have the seed of God inside us. The focus of God when man was to be made was, "I want a man that will reflect me on the earth, I want a man in my image, I want a man that will picture and capture my character," God created man with the seed of heaven, implying that if two people fashioned in his image live together as husband and wife, the world would be transformed into a glorious explosion. See Genesis 2:25 And they were both naked, the man and his wife, and were not ashamed. They were not ashamed because of the glory bestowed upon them. Two images of God were in the garden, and two glories of God were playing together in the garden; they had no reason to be ashamed. That is why the devil's first act was to ensure that man lost his glory and felt ashamed on the same day; we will discuss this in Chapter two.

Marriage is a weapon of war in the hands of God. How did I know this? See Psalm 127:3-5 Lo, children are an heritage of the Lord: and the fruit of the womb is His reward.

[4] As arrows are in the hand of a mighty man; so are children of the youth.

[5] Happy is the man that hath his quiver full of them: they shall not be ashamed, but they shall speak with the enemies in the gate.

I must expose these for us to understand why the devil is against homes, and this will help you determine the best weapon to employ in your marriage. We are all God's children, and he has sent us to the earth to fight the devil and his agents out of every area they have inhabited and to possess places for God, but how would a toxic home accomplish this? How can a home that has lost the key to God's glory accomplish this? This is why many homes are struggling today; they entered into marriage holding fast to the promises of God, and they prayed before they met at the altar, but they couldn't cope; the husband refuses to listen, the wife refuses to submit, the children are rebellious, and the marriage has evolved into a war zone.

Divorce and separation were not in God's original plan because man was not created to beat or abuse his wife. They were both naked and not ashamed, which means they do things together; they love, they dwell in glory, and there was no need for separation because they find joy and fulfillment in what they do.

I pray for you and every home under the attack of the devil; I command the peace of the living God; I send God's powerful hand to intervene in Jesus' name; and I destroy every stronghold of the devil in and around your home in Jesus' name.

THE DEVIL'S PLAN

Chapter Two

Let us pray: Father, I ask that you will expose the works of the devil as we check together the damage the devil has wreaked on homes in Jesus' name.

I want to encourage you to pray because God will be opening your eyes to some of the devil's secrets. This book is not intended to encourage divorce, though we will discuss it later. It is intended to combat the devil's attacks on homes and the devil's control over spouses who are toxic to each other.

We can see the traces of the devil's attack in the book of Genesis chapter three, but before we check it, I would want us to check why the devil came to attack.

Ezekiel 28:12-14 How art thou fallen from heaven, O Lucifer, son of the morning! How art thou cut down to the ground, which didst weaken the nations!

13 For thou hast said in thine heart, I will ascend into heaven, I will exalt my throne above the stars of God: I will sit also upon the mount of the congregation, in the sides of the north:

14 I will ascend above the heights of the clouds; I will be like the most High.

I want us to explore two points in these verses. The devil's objective was to be like God; his intention was also to take God's throne, but he forgot that angels were not created to attain that level, which is what drove him out of heaven. When man was to be made, see what God said in Genesis 1:26-27 And God said, Let us make man in our image, after our likeness: and let them have dominion over the fish of the sea, and over the fowl of the air, and over the cattle, and over all the earth, and over every creeping thing that creepeth upon the earth."

[27] So God created man in his image, in the image of God created He him; male and female created He them.

The devil wanted to be like God, so he was cast out of heaven, and now here comes a man made in God's image. To the devil, having an entity made in God's image is an insult, so he promised to fight the man until the glory of God is taken from him. Don't forget that when the devil fights a man, he is fighting a home. Every negative event in the family today is an inspiration from the pit of hell; the devil is the thief who comes to steal, slaughter, and destroy; he wishes for no home to exist because he is scared of the husband and wife's combined forces.

Secondly, the devil's rage over man and marriage was sparked by the fact that the devil had already been chased out of heaven to the earth before man was handed the key to the earth to control and conquer. Check out these scriptures, Revelation 12:12-13 Therefore rejoice, ye heavens, and ye that dwell in them. Woe to the inhabiters of the earth and of the sea! For the devil is come down unto you, having great wrath, because he knoweth that he hath but a short time.

[13] And when the dragon saw that he was cast unto the earth, he persecuted the woman which brought forth the man child.

I also remember in the scripture when John the Apostle was writing to the seven churches, he said something that always remembers

Revelation 2:13 I know thy works, and where thou dwellest, even where Satan's seat is

The day I read this scripture, it gave me an understanding of the devil's operation on the earth, and I am sorry to inform you that the devil has established his seat of power in different cities and homes, which is why you don't have to go far to see the devil's work. Imagine two friends killing themselves because of a chair. You may be wondering what a chair has to do with life.
This scripture will help
Roman 6:16 Know ye not, that to whom ye yield yourselves servants to obey, his servants ye are to whom ye obey; whether of sin unto death, or of obedience unto righteousness?

Do you realize that many times we know and observe that what is happening is the devil's plan, but we act or react wrongly? This is what ends many families today.

The devil was chased down to earth when he lost his place in heaven, and God made man rule over the devil's dwelling. When God saw the darkness on the earth in Genesis chapter 1:2-5 And the earth was without form, and void; and darkness was upon the face of the deep. And the Spirit of God moved upon the face of the waters.

³ And God said, Let there be light: and there was light.

⁴ And God saw the light, that it was good: and God divided the light from the darkness.

⁵ And God called the light Day, and the darkness he called Night. And the evening and the morning were the first day.

God commanded light into existence, which represents Jesus, but that didn't stop darkness from operating; it just set a limit to how far darkness could work. In verse four, the darkness mentioned there represents the devil, who was on the earth before man was created. Let us paraphrase that scripture this way: " Look, the devil is still on the earth because he cannot die, but wherever you see his work, dismantle it, chase him out, create a boundary, uproot it." He has given you the power to do so, which is why, as Christians, the next thing He exposes us to is power; For as many as received him, he gave them power to become God's sons, power to establish God's kingdom, power to advance, and power to cast the devil back into hell.

See what God did after making man, Genesis 1:28–30. And God blessed them, and God said unto them, Be fruitful and multiply, and replenish the earth, and subdue it: and have dominion over the fish of the sea, and over the fowl of the air, and over every living thing that moveth upon the earth.

²⁹ And God said, Behold, I have given you every herb bearing seed, which is upon the face of all the earth, and every tree, in the which is the fruit of a tree yielding seed; to you it shall be for meat.

³⁰ And to every beast of the earth, and to every fowl of the air, and to every thing that creepeth upon the earth, wherein there is life, I have given every green herb for meat: and it was so.

After the earth was created, God gave the key to man, which I believe is a double blow to the devil because, first, man is made in God's image, and second, God is giving man the key to the earth where the devil lives, and the devil began to plot how to bring the man down, how to thwart God's plan for man. The devil began looking for a way to make the man fall like himself, making it difficult to achieve what God intended for man to be.

How did we get here? Remember, when we talk about man, we're talking about home, about family, and the reason family was involved was to protect the eternal seed and blessing that God had bestowed upon man. I'll go into more detail on it in Chapter 3. Please remember, we're here to pray, and don't leave this chapter without prayer; stand on your guard now, evacuate, and destroy every appearance of the devil in your home and family. See this scripture, 1 John 3:8 He that committeth sin is of the devil; for the devil sinneth from the beginning. For this purpose the Son of God was manifested, that He might destroy the works of the devil. Congratulations if you are a child of God; if not, you may become one right now and stand in your position to demolish everything the adversary has assembled against your home. As we continue to reveal this secret in the next chapter, please pray and pray until you see answers to your prayers. Command your wife to submit to the knowledge of Christ, demand your husband to surrender to the knowledge of Christ, and command your children to submit to the knowledge of Christ. The devil is defrauding homes because he knows we are asleep, we have failed to take responsibility, and many homes are crumbling in our days. Let's rise together and chase that devil from our homes.

DEVIL AND THE FIRST HOME

Chapter Three

I hope you've been blessed as we've been revealing the devil's strategy from Chapter Two. We'll pick up where we left off: I want you to know why the devil focused his wrath on the first home and why he went through the woman.

The blessing to reproduce and multiply was put in man as a custodian of God's prophecy over the earth, as well as the divine seed. This means that, according to God's design, the more we multiply, the more the covenant of blessings over Adam expands, and the more we spread, the greater the light expands and drives out the devil. This is why the devil was pursuing man; he didn't want God's generational seed to be preserved. So he came up with a plan to penetrate the first home through the serpent. Genesis 3:1 Now the serpent was more subtil than any beast of the field which the Lord God had made. And he said unto the woman, Yea, hath God said, Ye shall not eat of every tree of the garden? Was the serpent the devil? No, the serpent was living in the garden with Adam and Eve, and because the devil couldn't get access to their lives and nothing could be done without it, he chose to employ the serpent. Eve failed to notice that the voice had changed, that it was no longer the same serpent living with them, and that the serpent had been possessed. This is what has brought many homes down and turned a happy home into a toxic environment. The boss had no idea that the secretary had been possessed by the devil; her voice had changed, but he didn't notice until he slept with her in the office. Many lives have been taken, and many homes have been damaged as a result of this. A friend of yesterday becomes an enemy of today; a saviour of yesterday becomes a disaster of today; that is why sensitivity is required in the home. Not every piece of information you should share with visitors, the covenant of blessing was given to men, not animals; why should the serpent be inquiring about what God said? Many toxic homes originated from knowledge that a stranger heard, space provided to a stranger, or a gift received from a stranger. If we don't rise, the devil will continue to struggle against the seed of man even to this day.

See again, Genesis 3: 4-6 [4] And the serpent said unto the woman, Ye shall not surely die:

[5] For God doth know that in the day ye eat thereof, then your eyes shall be opened, and ye shall be as gods, knowing good and evil.

[6] And when the woman saw that the tree was good for food, and that it was pleasant to the eyes, and a tree to be desired to make one wise, she took of the fruit thereof, and did eat, and gave also unto her husband with her; and he did eat.

The devil created a friendship between the serpent and the woman, and the serpent could even advise her. Moreover, Adam was not sensitive enough to notice that something strange was going on; the Bible confirmed that Adam was with her. How come the spiritual transaction was going on while the custodian of the divine mandate was sleeping? The door of his home had been opened to a stranger. Since the serpent became their friend, it was impossible to hear the voice of God again; it was just the devil speaking through the serpent, and they began to consider the devil's advice. You must stand over your home and close all spiritual doors that have been opened for strangers to enter. You must chase out the demon and seal the door against it because you have been given the authority to do so.

Psalm 18:44-45 As soon as they hear of me, they shall obey me: the strangers shall submit themselves unto me. [45] The strangers shall fade away, and be afraid out of their close places.

You may either choose to stand or do nothing; whatever character you portray in your home is sponsored by God or the devil; roar like a lion, talk as the sons and daughters of the most high, and let the devil's stronghold be destroyed.

Don't forget where we started; the devil recognized that home is one of the factors that will ensure that God's commanded generational blessings are preserved; the more we spread, the stronger the covenant; and the devil recognized that if a man eats the forbidden fruit, he will die and that when he gives birth, he will not be able to give birth in the covenant of the blessing but in the deadness of the spirit; this is what happened; let us check the scripture:

Genesis 3:6-8 And when the woman saw that the tree was good for food, that it was pleasant to the eyes, and a tree to be desired to make one wise, she took of the fruit thereof, and did eat, and gave also unto her husband with her; and he did eat. [7] And the eyes of them both were opened, and they knew that they were naked; and they sewed fig leaves together, and made themselves aprons.

[8] And they heard the voice of the Lord God walking in the garden in the cool of the day: and Adam and his wife hid themselves from the presence of the Lord God amongst the trees of the garden.

They ate the fruit after much persuasion by the devil. Let me say this: you may be sleeping, but the devil does not; if he fails on one side, he will enter through the other door; the best thing is to keep your guard up. They plummeted from the pinnacle of heavenly blessing, from the dwelling of God's presence, and they sank without control through the devil. The first thing they noticed was that they were naked. They have been naked since the beginning. Something covered them, the glory of God, the presence of the Father—because they were filled with all of God and the manifestation of His presence, and they lost it in a flash. They now use leaves in place of God's glory, and the leaves couldn't even cover all of them.

Hosea 8:3 ³ Israel hath cast off the thing that is good: the enemy shall pursue him.

When a home or a man loses God's presence, they are in the devil's presence. It is easier for the devil to manipulate homes without Christ than homes with Christ. What is the situation in your home? Have you lost God's glory? Have you given the devil a foothold? You can rewrite the story today.

The second thing that happened to them was that they were ashamed. They couldn't meet with God when He came to visit because they had lost the key to His presence; they had left the position that God placed them. Don't play games with the devil; you can't win; his game was well planned and executed; a man can live his life however he wants, but the devil cannot. Man used to live with God's inspiration, but the devil now has access to man's heart; this is the foundation of a toxic home, where you see people misbehaving in the home for no apparent reason; however, you can stand as a watchman, chasing out that devil, who has taken possession of your home and your spouse's character thus far.

What happened after the fall of man is of concern to us, check it out.

Genesis 4:3-8 And in process of time it came to pass, that Cain brought of the fruit of the ground an offering unto the Lord.

⁴ And Abel, he also brought of the firstlings of his flock and of the fat thereof. And the Lord had respect unto Abel and to his offering:

⁵ But unto Cain and to his offering he had not respect. And Cain was very wroth, and his countenance fell.

⁶ And the Lord said unto Cain, Why art thou wroth? and why is thy countenance fallen?

⁷ If thou doest well, shalt thou not be accepted? and if thou doest

not well, sin lieth at the door. And unto thee shall be his desire, and thou shalt rule over him.

[8] And Cain talked with Abel his brother: and it came to pass, when they were in the field, that Cain rose against Abel his brother, and slew him.

What happened in the scriptural passage above is a reflection of Adam and Eve's life after the fall; Cain's heart factor was corrupted to the point where God couldn't accept his offering; no one had ever killed before him, but the devil whispered to him, "Why don't you kill your brother because God loves him more than you," and he accepted it without remorse; this was exactly what the devil wanted; how can someone living in disobedience preserve the generational blessing and covenant? The children who would have kept the blessings have become killers, and because the devil realized that God was delighted with Abel, he knew he could keep the mandate, so, he was slain. The devil has meticulously planned his strategy; he wants the children to be raised entirely by a murderer in order for them to be inspired by him and corrupted. What is happening among today's youths is a mirror of the family where many of them grew up. Mummy and Daddy couldn't pray together anymore; there was no intimacy; they were living as neighbors in the same house, and they had no idea they were planting a seed in their children's lives.

You can command that habit out of your home, that demon out of your marriage; you can stand as one and maintain the generational blessings received through Jesus. The devil has tricked you enough, let him know your home is not an option. Rise as Deborah and possess every land occupied by the devil.

THE FORBIDDEN FRUIT

Chapter Four

Genesis 2:16-17 And the Lord God commanded the man, saying, Of every tree of the garden thou mayest freely eat: 17 But of the tree of the knowledge of good and evil, thou shalt not eat of it: for in the day that thou eatest thereof thou shalt surely die.

Man's life is full of many things, and sometimes he seeks things he doesn't need. God told Adam that he might eat from any tree in the garden except one in the middle and that if he eats it, he would die. The fruit on this tree is the forbidden fruit we will be examining in this chapter. The consequence alone is enough to make a man flee; the devil has fooled man into loving what God despises; this is the beginning of man's downfall. The devil's first target is man's spirit; everything that happens in the physical begins in the spirit long before it happens in the physical; this is why family sensitivity is necessary. No man can fall physically unless he has first fallen spiritually; such a man has in some way or another exposed himself to the forbidden fruit and caused havoc in his spiritual life, thereby disconnecting him from God, and the devil will begin to whisper to him on how to behave, and whatever the devil says will be carried out. This is why I am personally against Christians watching secular movies; the risk to our souls is too great. Many husbands have been caught on the altar of fornication as a result of what they were exposed to; and unfortunately, eighty per cent of comedy skits on social media in this age is about a lady with a big breast, naked stomach, shaking buttocks, and this is what one man has exposed himself to for days. After he has even stopped watching, the video continues to loop in his subconscious mind until he dances to the game's rhythm. Many powerful men have fallen victim to this trap.

How to know if your partner has eaten a forbidden fruit is when you consider he has withdrawn his love for God. Let us check the scripture, Matthew 24:12 [12] And because iniquity shall abound, the love of many shall wax cold.

No one can taste the forbidden fruit and stay in God's presence. The fruit will always chase him away; such a spouse will no longer spend quality time before God as he once did; he will find it difficult to do the things he was fervently doing for God. When you consider that your spouse has been exposed to the fruit and is injured, the next step is to launch a rescue mission, which I will discuss later.

The worst mistake couple usually may make is when one party eats a forbidden fruit and the other party, who is supposed to save the first, eats it as well. See this scripture again, Genesis 3:6 And when the woman saw that the tree was good for food, and that it was pleasant to the eyes, and a tree to be desired to make one wise, she took of the fruit thereof, and did eat, and gave also unto her husband with her; and he did eat.

If Adam had stood in his position, he would have rescued his wife, but he replied to his wife's gift of forbidden fruit by agreeing to die with her, and they both died. How many times have you agreed to die with your spouse because you thought it would solve the problem? You became upset with her when she was angry. She wanted to fight with you, and you also claimed you enjoy fighting, the more you do this, the more you destroy your home.

See Galatians 6:17-21 For the flesh lusteth against the Spirit, and the Spirit against the flesh: and these are contrary the one to the other: so that ye cannot do the things that ye would. [18] But if ye be led of the Spirit, ye are not under the law. [19] Now the works of the flesh are manifest, which are these; Adultery, fornication, uncleanness, lasciviousness,

[20] Idolatry, witchcraft, hatred, variance, emulations, wrath, strife, seditions, heresies,

[21] Envyings, murders, drunkenness, revellings, and such like: of the which I tell you before, as I have also told you in time past, that they which do such things shall not inherit the kingdom of God.

Please don't play the game with the devi. If a demon whispers any of these to your spouse; you can only manage things when you're in the Spirit, but if you let loose, you'll say more than you are expected to say. You will say what you don't want to say, you will react like an unbeliever, never take the offer of the forbidden fruit from your spouse, never allow him to draw you into the grave of death he has dug, you may not survive it. Never prove a point when he is out of point, your point won't make sense, when your spouse is out of control, it will show in his actions and words; at that point, ask for grace and be under the control of the Spirit. Your flesh will suggest you accept your spouse's offer; your flesh will suggest you respond harshly to him; the devil will tell you that you are not a slave, just one small response from you will set the home on fire, and you may not live to see the end of it. If you had been quiet, if you had walked away, it might not have happened. I understand that people value honour over dishonour, and I understand how it feels to be dishonoured by a spouse who should honour you; however, be sensitive and recognise that it is no longer your spouse who is speaking; it is anger, pride, and arrogance, the instrument sent by the devil to destroy your home and the forbidden fruit sent by the devil to render God's plan useless in your home. What the devil wants is for you to accept the offer, because if you do, the two of you will die, and you won't be able to pray together, study the Bible together, or sleep together again. One thing you don't realise is that, if you fight him for abusing you, you haven't dealt with the spirit behind it, and it will only make the devil happier.

Dear spouse, never accept any offer from the devil, and if one of you does by accident, do not fall with him; instead, grasp his hand and help him up. Let us consider this scripture:

[9] Two are better than one; because they have a good reward for their labour.

[10] For if they fall, the one will lift up his fellow: but woe to him that is alone when he falleth; for he hath not another to help him up.

[11] Again, if two lie together, then they have heat: but how can one be warm alone?

[12] And if one prevail against him, two shall withstand him; and a threefold cord is not quickly broken. Ecclesiastes 4:9-12

You can only lift him when you are standing, but it will be difficult if you have also fallen. Be aware that your home is unique, and the devil will fight it. Prepare ahead of time, and I pray that anyone falling in your home receives strength now. Your home is restored, and your peace is restored in Jesus' name.

SEPARATED TO BE ELIMINATED

CHAPTER FIVE

Separation is the quickest method for the devil to convert a lovely home into a toxic home; please read attentively as I expose you to certain things we consider ordinary in the home. See the scripture:

Genesis 2:24 24 Therefore shall a man leave his father and his mother, and shall cleave unto his wife: and they shall be one flesh. The first golden rule given by God after Eve was brought to Adam was to cleave. The Lord knew that any little space between husband and wife could lead to the breakdown of the home, so He told them to cleave together. I'm not saying it won't happen, but it will be hard to break apart homes that are bound together because their pains and burdens are shared together.

I'd like us to consider the story of Judas in the Bible:
Luke 22: Now the feast of unleavened bread drew nigh, which is called the Passover.

2 And the chief priests and scribes sought how they might kill him; for they feared the people.

3 Then entered Satan into Judas surnamed Iscariot, being of the

number of the twelve.

4 And he went his way, and communed with the chief priests and captains, how he might betray him unto them.

5 And they were glad, and covenanted to give him money.

6 And he promised, and sought opportunity to betray him unto them in the absence of the multitude.

Because Satan lacks the strength to penetrate a man who is united with his brothers, he will first separate him; he may take years to gain a foothold before striking his target. According to what was written, Judas has not been consistent in his relationship with Jesus, which is why the devil was able to easily gain access to his life; he has no one among the disciples to discuss it with. He proceeded directly to carry out the devil's demand since his heart was far from Jesus. Do you know that even after the elders' consent, he took days before betraying Jesus, yet he didn't repent because the devil was now his companion to kill him, he was separated to be eliminated.

Cleaving is an assignment that must be done deliberately by the couple; it will always be difficult if it is done by one party, as the other may not appreciate it and may break the home. Cleaving is a journey that begins with our actions and interactions after marriage. After our wedding, I became conscious of how I interact with my wife and swore not to change. I enjoy doing anything that makes my family happy and brings us all together.

We have a high divorce rate today because intimacy is now a story in the home. None of them knows what each party is going through, and it is reflecting in their actions and affecting everything about the home.

How come the best couple can still separate? How come they can't live together again? How come they don't want to see themselves again? How come they've decided to file for divorce? The devil got a foothold because of the offense they couldn't solve. When they started having children, the love of one shifted to the child because they couldn't sleep together again. When it is more convenient to separate rooms and live alone, keep an eye on it; the heart is gradually separating.

If you're reading this and your home is toxic as a result of a lack of intimacy, go back to your spouse; Nothing can be accomplished unless you're together; rebuild your home; nothing should cause you to be toxic to each other; whatever you don't have will be provided by God; it's not enough to create a space.

Let me state unequivocally that the wreckage that follows separation in the home is not always good; many parents have abandoned their children to go their ways; the devil aims to eliminate you; the devil's purpose is to murder your home. Don't give the devil your home because of your character; instead, go back to your lover and keep yourself together; the storm will soon be over. It's phase.

CONFLICT MANAGEMENT

This chapter will be devoted to marital conflict management. I want to emphasize that you should not regard your home as an afterthought; it is a priority. You should not have another plan for your home, believing that you can leave at any point if things don't work out; the fact is that the way you handle your home will show in your actions. Many young couples in this generation are no longer committed to marriage; they constantly want to leave because of minor misunderstandings caused by their egos that can be resolved; however, permit me to point out that the same conflict that broke some homes was managed by another. According to Hebrews 12:1, ...we are surrounded by cloud of witnesses. So, you have no excuse. You must learn to work out your marriage.

When you see a couple celebrating fifty or sixty years of marriage, how do you feel about it? They are not only celebrating the happiness and joy of marriage, but they are also celebrating years of joy together, tears together, misunderstandings that didn't break them, storms that came but didn't kill them, and many other hidden stories in their marriage. We will continue to have broken homes until we understand that home is not for boys and until we learn conflict management. I am afraid of the kind of society we will have in the future when two people from broken homes marry, it is better imagined. It wasn't this bad in the beginning, but the more we advance, the more difficult it becomes. Social media is not helping matters, and this is what we have been exposed to.

I had the privilege of counselling some ladies from the Philippines two years ago; they were single mothers, and they made me realize that the rate of broken homes in that country is extremely high. We have forgotten that God instituted home. Don't get me wrong; some situations may warrant the couple to separate for a time, which I will discuss later, but it must not become a doctrine. Until we recognize that we are at war with the devil, he will continue to win over families. The worst aspect is that marriages lasting two to six months are crumbling. I mourn for this generation, and all I can do is pray that God will intervene and show compassion in Jesus' name.

Conflict in marriage is part of marriage, and it is what intending couples should prepare for before getting married. Many things can cause conflict because our exposure is different, our backgrounds are different, and these are two people from different families coming together. The husband will want things done the way he does with his parents; the wife will want things done the way she does with her parents; and because neither of them wants to give in, it will always end in misunderstanding. The sincere truth is that the essence of misunderstanding is to build you into perfection; stop seeing it as a strange thing. Ask for grace, and God will help you in Jesus' name. We shall consider the scripture:

Colossians 3:13-24 [13] Forbearing one another and forgiving one another, if any man have a quarrel against any: even as Christ forgave you, so also do ye.

[14] And above all these things put on charity, which is the bond of

perfectness.

15 And let the peace of God rule in your hearts, to the which also ye are called in one body; and be ye thankful.

16 Let the word of Christ dwell in you richly in all wisdom; teaching and admonishing one another in psalms and hymns and spiritual songs, singing with grace in your hearts to the Lord.

17 And whatsoever ye do in word or deed, do all in the name of the Lord Jesus, giving thanks to God and the Father by him.

18 Wives, submit yourselves unto your own husbands, as it is fit in the Lord.

19 Husbands, love your wives, and be not bitter against them.

20 Children, obey your parents in all things: for this is well pleasing unto the Lord.

21 Fathers, provoke not your children to anger, lest they be discouraged.

22 Servants, obey in all things your masters according to the flesh; not with eyeservice, as menpleasers; but in singleness of heart, fearing God;

23 And whatsoever ye do, do it heartily, as to the Lord, and not unto men;

24 Knowing that of the Lord ye shall receive the reward of the inheritance: for ye serve the Lord Christ.

We shall be considering some points mentioned in the Bible passages above:

Forbearing and forgiving one another: The truth is that if you can't let go, you can't forgive, and it may be difficult to live in peace at home. It appears that forgiveness is now forbidden in homes in this generation. We count on little things, and we'll be looking for a way to take vengeance. We usually think that vengeance will make him feel the pain we're feeling, but this isn't true. Vengeance escalates issues beyond control. Another point to consider is that we must forgive as Christ has forgiven us; thus, if we are to consider the forgiveness required of us, we must also consider Christ's forgiveness of the church. Matthew 18:21-22 Then came Peter to him, and said, Lord, how oft shall my brother sin against me, and I forgive him? till seven times?

²² Jesus saith unto him, I say not unto thee, Until seven times: but, Until seventy times seven.

Forgiveness, according to Jesus, can only be recorded for a day and must not be recalled the following day. Offences of yesterday should not be referred to today. This is why forbearance is so important; we cannot build a prosperous home if we cannot bear with one another.

Proverb17:9 He that covereth a transgression seeketh love; but he that repeateth a matter separateth very friends.

Prepare your heart for this knowledge, and it will help your home. The Lord wants us to forgive and forbear. The verse confirms that He died for us while we were still sinners. When two people come together and refuse to learn because they are consumed by their egos, or when one comes to build when the other has no idea why he married, the home becomes cancerous. This is why it is critical to get it right. If you know someone who has never married and wants to get it right, I recommend the book "Life, Purpose, and Marriage," which I co-authored with my wife. Please buy it for them; it will help them prepare for the long journey of marriage.

Charity, the bond of perfection: Remember, we're checking the points raised by the scripture about conflict management; another word for charity is "love." The scripture is emphasizing that you cannot be perfected if you don't love; you can only love with your heart, which is why if you don't love, it will show. Love is unconditional, not because he is the best or because she is the most beautiful, but because love creates an unending bond in the home. To make your home function, love demands sacrifice, including time and other resources. Here are several passages from the Bible that deal with love:

1Peter 4: ⁸ And above all things have fervent charity among yourselves: for charity shall cover the multitude of sins.

John 15:12-13 ¹² This is my commandment, That ye love one another as I have loved you.

¹³ Greater love hath no man than this, that a man lay down his life for his friends.

Ephesians 4:2-3 ² With all lowliness and meekness, with longsuffering, forbearing one another in love;

³ Endeavouring to keep the unity of the Spirit in the bond of peace.

It will be difficult to sacrifice for someone you do not love, which is why I will encourage you to be bound by love. Do not allow the devil's assault to compromise your love for your spouse; instead, stay firm and combat the demon who is invading your home.

Let the peace of God rule in your heart: Let me say this clearly: never lose your peace for the sake of your spouse. The absence of peace is the beginning of a storm; the absence of peace is the beginning of fear and anxiety; the absence of peace is the beginning of sorrow; never allow your heart to be troubled; instead, ask God for help, and I am confident that He will. Many arrows will be shot against your peace in marriage; many married women die before their time because they let go of their peace at a certain point in time because of a report they heard about their spouse. They trusted and relied on him, and he disappointed them; as a result, many of them chose not to live their lives again and died in a mess. Please, keep your peace! See the scripture:

Philippians 4:6-7 Be careful for nothing; but in everything by prayer and supplication with thanksgiving let your requests be made known unto God.

⁷ And the peace of God, which passeth all understanding, shall keep your hearts and minds through Christ Jesus.

The biblical passages above highlight something I'd want to speak on: "be concerned about nothing, pray about everything." The devil has now changed it for us: we're worried about everything and praying about nothing, which is why our peace is threatened. Don't let the devil steal your peace; be deliberate about preserving it. Never lose your peace; it will keep your heart safe from unforgiveness and revenge.

Let the word of Christ dwell in you richly: This will be the last point in this chapter, as we shall be considering the rest of the points as we continue in this book. The word of God is one thing that generates quick internal strength against external storms. One perfect plan of the devil is to keep the home too busy to study the word of God so that he can attack the home. The more you dwell on the word, the more strength you will have to fight the devil. Never be too busy to study the word. See the scripture,

2Timothy 3:16-17 [16] All scripture is given by inspiration of God, and is profitable for doctrine, for reproof, for correction, for instruction in righteousness:

[17] That the man of God may be perfect, thoroughly furnished unto all good works.

Joshua 1:8 This book of the law shall not depart out of thy mouth; but thou shalt meditate therein day and night, that thou mayest observe to do according to all that is written therein: for then thou shalt make thy way prosperous, and then thou shalt have good success.

The devil's secret will be revealed through the word of God, and you will be disciplined and warned until you are perfected. The more you meditate on God's word, the more strength you will get. The word of God will prepare you for events that may occur in your home. The word of God will advise you; the word of God will cause you to stand firm, but, living outside the word means exposing yourself to life's storms.

I will love to talk about this system I learned about from the virtuous woman in the book of Proverbs.

Proverb 31: [26] She openeth her mouth with wisdom; and in her tongue is the law of kindness.

This was a woman who had been filled with the word of God, and she knew the proper thing to say at the right moment. One prayer point that spouses should pray for is for God to provide them with the the wisdom needed to handle each other. Many wives do not know how to treat their husbands, and vice versa. You need wisdom; you don't tackle problems the way they are. No amount of anger can solve a problem; only peace can. No amount of unforgiveness can solve a problem; only forgiveness can. No foolishness can solve a problem; only wisdom can. Ask the Lord to help you, and He will in Jesus' name.

CONFLICT FIRST AID

After we have checked conflict management, we must check the weapon to use when conflict arises. Many broken homes today would not have been broken if they had understood this; yet, in a case where both parties desire to stand on their rights, such a home will find it difficult to stand. I recall what my father told me about 25 years ago, when he said, "Learn to say sorry whether you are right or wrong," and it has stayed with me to this day, and has enabled me to resolve several conflicts that might otherwise have escalated. Proverb 15:1-2 A soft answer turneth away wrath, but grievous words stir up anger. 2 The tongue of the wise uses knowledge aright: but the mouth of fools poureth out foolishness.

In homes, how we handle conflicts matters; The same mouth that stirred up fury could now be used to calm situations; it all depends on how it is used. A conflict that is not effectively handled can jeopardize the joy of the family; this is why we must analyze how we respond to conflict anytime we encounter it.

I recall my wife calling me at work to remind me to get something when coming home, and she'd be upset if I didn't, and that was the first thing she would address before welcoming me home. This was a challenge in my home for a while until she recognized the fact that she needed to change, and since then, she would welcome me home. In some situations where I forgot to buy what she needed, i would have to sacrifice to go and get it.

We shall be discussing some points that can help against conflict **Prepare your heart that offence will come**: One thing that will assist your home is for you to prepare your heart for your partner's offence. Believe me when I say that we often respond more than the offence because we haven't prepared for it. Remember that you are marrying a human being, not God; pray for God's guidance, you may not be able to do it on your own, but with His help, it can be easy. Keep in mind that you have no choice but to be in your marriage; thus, be prepared for your spouse's faults. This does not imply you have made a mistake marrying him; rather, his mistakes may help you better understand him and also yourself. It will also help you to identify prayer points.

Realize the problem: In my research, I discovered that some homes are toxic today because the husband and wife fail to discuss past offences. Whenever one of the spouses offends the other, they simply give it time and move on without talking or apologizing about it. Such a home cannot work because one spouse is wounded while the other moves freely. Because one party is not free from the covered offence, it will be replayed brutally. **Note that any offence you fail to address today will soon develop into a weapon of war in the devil's hands against your home tomorrow.** Never act as if you aren't aware of an offence when it occurred; whenever you notice a change in your partner, call him or her and inquire as to what the problem is. Try as much as you can to not let go until the issue is resolved, and try as much as you can to avoid such things repeating themselves. Saying sorry is not a sign of weakness, but of strength. Please recognize and apply whatever resolves conflict in your house. Always be a peacekeeper in your family; your spouse may not know it now, but he will one day, and you will be vindicated.

Never allow your emotion to do the talk: When an offence takes place, it is common for us to allow our emotions to speak for us. This is when you remember how you suffered for him, how you helped him pay his debt and the pain of a nine-month pregnancy. If you have not put your emotions under control, anger will use it and cause negative effects that you will live to regret. I heard a story of a housewife who broke her husband's iPad because of a misunderstanding. I'd want to point out that unless you learn to control your emotions, you won't be able to predict the chaos you will cause. Many born-again Christians have lost their homes as a result of an eruption of emotion that was out of control, and many humble people have lost their treasured things as a result of emotion bringing forth wrath that they couldn't manage.

Moses' story in the Bible is one that I will never forget; he gave everything, suffered many things, endured many insults, and he interceded all the way. Nobody knew he was an angry man until the day he couldn't control his emotion, he was emotionally attached to the situation, and anger rose in him. See the scripture:

Number 20: ² And there was no water for the congregation: and they gathered themselves together against Moses and against Aaron.

³ And the people chode with Moses, and spake, saying, Would God that we had died when our brethren died before the Lord!

⁴ And why have ye brought up the congregation of the Lord into this wilderness, that we and our cattle should die there?

⁵ And wherefore have ye made us to come up out of Egypt, to bring us in unto this evil place? it is no place of seed, or of figs, or of vines, or of pomegranates; neither is there any water to drink.

⁶ And Moses and Aaron went from the presence of the assembly unto the door of the tabernacle of the congregation, and they fell upon their faces: and the glory of the Lord appeared unto them.

⁷ And the Lord spake unto Moses, saying, ⁸ Take the rod, and gather thou the assembly together, thou, and Aaron thy brother, and

speak ye unto the rock before their eyes; and it shall give forth his water, and thou shalt bring forth to them water out of the rock: so thou shalt give the congregation and their beasts drink.

⁹ And Moses took the rod from before the Lord, as he commanded him.

¹⁰ And Moses and Aaron gathered the congregation together before the rock, and he said unto them, Hear now, ye rebels; must we fetch you water out of this rock?

¹¹ And Moses lifted up his hand, and with his rod he smote the rock twice: and the water came out abundantly, and the congregation drank, and their beasts also.

¹² And the Lord spake unto Moses and Aaron, Because ye believed me not, to sanctify me in the eyes of the children of Israel, therefore ye shall not bring this congregation into the land which I have given them.

You may have many reasons to respond, and many reasons to act; he may have been repeating it and failing to repent; consider the harm you will cause, and the lives you will negatively influence. Who could have guessed that Moses' mere actions would cost him the Promised Land? It's a pity that many families that started out strong, built on the foundation of Jesus, have drifted apart, and those who remain together are no longer enjoying their marriage.

Will you not cry out to God and ask Him to deliver you from the emotions that have nearly destroyed your life? You may believe it is difficult, but not with God's help. See the scripture:

Matthew 19: ²³ Then said Jesus unto his disciples, Verily I say unto you, That a rich man shall hardly enter into the kingdom of heaven.

²⁴ And again I say unto you, It is easier for a camel to go through the eye of a needle, than for a rich man to enter into the kingdom of God.

²⁵ When his disciples heard it, they were exceedingly amazed,

saying, Who then can be saved?

26 But Jesus beheld them, and said unto them, With men this is impossible; but with God all things are possible.

It is possible with God if you can surrender all to Him and allow Him to take charge of your life, Never depend on your strength; a therapist can only try; help belongs to God, Cry to Him and help will come your way. The flesh will always fight the spirit until the end, and the flesh will always dictate a way of pulling down the spirit. Be guided; I see God helping you in Jesus' name.

Know when to talk and when not: If you can adopt this basic approach, it will help you achieve peace in your home. People talk when they are offended for two reasons: the first is that they want to prove a point, and the second is that they feel cheated. As valuable as these points are, if they are not correctly applied, they may shatter what you are trying to build. Proving a point in a tense situation does not always go well, because you will discover that your motive is also your partner's motive, and both of you will end up shouting at each other, and at the end of the day, nobody is willing to listen. You may believe you are right, but your partner claims to be right as well. The best thing to do is to be silent and wait for the right moment to say it. Be careful not to let the devil borrow your body to carry out his plan, or you will live to regret it, which is why you need God's wisdom in your home because you may not have another opportunity to prove your points. Let us check some Bible verses that will help us with this matter:

Ephesians 4:29 Let no corrupt communication proceed out of your mouth, but that which is good to the use of edifying, that it may minister grace unto the hearers.

Proverb 13:3 He that keepeth his mouth keepeth his life: but he that openeth wide his lips shall have destruction.

Proverb 10:19 In the multitude of words there wanteth not sin: but he that refraineth his lips is wise.

Proverb 15:23 A man hath joy by the answer of his mouth: and a

word spoken in due season, how good is it!
Proverb 15:1A soft answer turneth away wrath:
but grievous words stir up anger.
I have numerous biblical scriptures regarding this that I can't fit into this space. No matter how intelligent you are, if you talk when you don't have to, you will be considered a fool. I see God helping you in Jesus' name.

WHEN TO ALLOW THE THIRD PARTY

Chapter Eight

There is a statement that claims a third party should not be permitted in a marriage, which is entirely correct. However, many people have used this adage to injure their spouse, and since they know she would not speak up, they continue to maltreat and then murder her over time.

Allow me to state unequivocally that, whether your home is running smoothly or not, you are expected to have a spiritual head over you. Unfortunately, many spiritual orphans (someone without a spiritual head) are marrying these days, believing marriage will solve all of their problems, only to discover that marriage is an entirely new challenge. It doesn't matter whosoever has abused the office of the spiritual head, its place cannot be taken off when it comes to home and marriage.

If you are still single and have the opportunity to read this, please do not marry an orphan. There may come a time in your life when you will need someone to look after your home. Who will you contact, or will you go and create an emergency friend who will not be able to help your home?

Because this is a Christian book, I will base my response on biblical principles. My concept of a third party is as follows: The third party is the external body that is a member of the party. A third party is similar to a coach on the field; he does not play the ball, but he is an important member of the team. The third party is not an outsider or a stranger; the third party is someone who has been with you on your marital journey before you met. The third party's job is to pray with you, offer you advice, and keep an eye on you without intruding on your privacy. They don't talk about issues unless you bring them up, but they are always accessible. This is why I recommend your spiritual head.

My spiritual parents were with me throughout my marital journey; they became involved while I was getting ready, and they are still with me today. I don't want to be an orphan, and my wife knows whom to report me to if need be. We need to check the scripture here:

Ruth 3:1-8 Then Naomi her mother in law said unto her, My daughter, shall I not seek rest for thee, that it may be well with thee?

2 And now is not Boaz of our kindred, with whose maidens thou wast? Behold, he winnoweth barley to night in the threshingfloor.

3 Wash thyself therefore, and anoint thee, and put thy raiment upon thee, and get thee down to the floor: but make not thyself known unto the man, until he shall have done eating and drinking.

4 And it shall be, when he lieth down, that thou shalt mark the place where he shall lie, and thou shalt go in, and uncover his feet, and lay thee down; and he will tell thee what thou shalt do.

5 And she said unto her, All that thou sayest unto me I will do.

Ruth's mother-in-law was essential to her success; she acted as a spiritual and physical head over her, providing her with sound advice both before and after her marriage. May I inquire, Who do you submit to at this time? Who is it that provides advice? Who is the patriarch of your family? It is necessary to have a common parent, a mentor, and a spiritual adviser over your household, not specifically to settle disputes, but to provide guidance when needed.

After you've grasped the role of the third party, it's critical that you make your decision prayerfully and thoughtfully so that your home is not damaged in the process. The third party's job is to strengthen your home, not to harm it. Once you have this picture, you'll be able to determine whom to submit to. See one more scripture on this:

Ecclesiastes 4: [9] Two are better than one; because they have a good reward for their labour.

[10] For if they fall, the one will lift up his fellow: but woe to him that is alone when he falleth; for he hath not another to help him up.

[11] Again, if two lie together, then they have heat: but how can one be warm alone?

[12] And if one prevail against him, two shall withstand him; and a threefold cord is not quickly broken.

We see the weakness of standing alone, the strength of two people, and the unbroken strength of three. Many people assume that the third cord mentioned here is the Holy Spirit, which is correct, but if we break it down further, the third cord is often that faithful man watching over you. The man who is ready to give you sound advice at all times. We were fortunate to meet a family that served as a third cord for us after our wedding. They stayed by our side through thick and thin, and they are always willing to answer our questions about issues we don't understand.

For clarity, let me emphasize the points mentioned so far:
The term "third-party" refers to the position of the party's third member. He must be a member of the family and a partner in your struggle. You can't just choose a stranger to help you when you have a challenge, someone who hasn't been with you from onset.

Having stated that, you must choose when to bring a third party into your home, you must recognise that we cannot avoid misunderstandings in the home. I will divide this into two categories: minor misunderstandings and major misunderstandings. We will spend time discussing these:

Minor misunderstandings: These are the types of misunderstandings that we encounter daily, such as; when your partner fails to buy what you asked him to buy, when your partner forgets your anniversary day, when you promise something and forget it, when you shout at her by accident, and so on. These are minor offences in the home that, if not handled properly, can lead to major offences.

Major misunderstandings: These are caused by repeated offences for which there is no cause to repent. For example, as a Christian, your husband may have become a drunkard, womanizer, or other, and after apologizing the first time, he continues to do so, and he is getting highly toxic, It is important that you seek the advice of a third party of your home. Also, If your wife can nag on virtually everything or keep friends who are toxic to the family or playing immature about some issues, you need to involve a third party.

They will know how to contact him and convey the information wisely. Another important reason to involve a third party is sex. When you don't speak the same language about sex and one is sex starving, you need external intervention. This has led many Christian husbands to backslide, but I believe the right thing to do is to involve your family's third party, which is why I asked you to choose wisely and never die in silence on issues that can be resolved. I understand that involving them may not always result in a solution, especially if the issue has progressed to a critical stage before they are engaged. However, you will know that you have people who understand what you are going through and are praying for you. This is why you have to learn to speak up on time to avoid irreparable situation.

WHEN MARRIAGE IS LIFE-THREATENING

Chapter Nine

I purposefully left this point out of the last chapter because it deserves its own chapter. Many wives have been killed because their husbands are unable to control their anger and emotions. I heard a story about a young man who killed his newlywed wife and left her body at her parents' house. This is not God's purpose for families, which is why I encourage singles to read the book I co-authored with my wife, titled, 'Life, Purpose, and Marriage'.

One thing I want you to understand is that you got married because you had life; If you don't have life, you can't marry. I've never seen a church where they join dead bodies together; it hasn't happened and it won't happen. At this point, we can say that life is the vehicle that drives the marriage. You got married because you had life; if you don't have life again, you won't be able to marry, and that is why Apostle Paul says that, when one partner dies, the other is no longer bound by any covenant.

Roman 7:2-3 For the woman which hath a husband is bound by the law to her husband so long as he liveth; but if the husband be dead, she is loosed from the law of her husband.

³ So then if, while her husband liveth, she be married to another man, she shall be called an adulteress: but if her husband be dead, she is free from that law; so that she is no adulteress, though she be married to another man.

What we're trying to say is that you can only keep your marriage vows if you're alive, and you can only live as husband and wife if you're alive, which is why it's so crucial to keep that life that drives the marriage. If you have been driving a car for a long time and fail to maintain it, the automobile will eventually stop serving you and you will lose the joy of driving it, even if you will buy another one later. For the time being, you will suffer since you do not have one.

This is why it is necessary to maintain your life and never place your marriage above your life. Your reason for existence is not only about marriage. Many people are unaware of this and are killing their spouses. They are self-centred and do not care about what the other partner is going through. They graduate from bachelor to manchelor (a married man living like a bachelor); they are still living alone, making decisions alone, spending their income alone, and ruling like the king of the jungle.

This is for the husbands here; never put your marriage ahead of your wife. She is the meaning of marriage; she comes as your assistance; she must be preserved. See what the Bible says about your wife:

Proverb 18:22 ²² Whoso findeth a wife findeth a good thing, and obtaineth favour of the Lord.

Two points are given here as to why you can't maltreat your wife in any case, why you can't incapacitate your wife, and why your wife, not your children, must be your first concern. Your wife is a good thing and a favour from God, according to the Bible, and comprehending this will cause you to cherish her and hold her in love and appreciate her.

My five years of marriage have been fantastic, I love her even more than when I first met her. Her body is still precious to me; I am still moved by her nakedness. She is becoming more beautiful to me daily. I still carry her as I did five years ago. I still sing to her, and, most importantly, I speak positively to her every single day; I speak what I want her life to be, I speak to her beauty and her purpose; it's no surprise she is finding fulfilment under my roof. Did you know I can decide to act the other way round? I can decide to make our love fade away. I can decide to make the house unhealthy, but NO! I determine how I want my home to be, whatever picture you see in your home is chosen by you and you can change it if you want.

Here we shall discuss things that make the marriage to be life-threatening:

When the spouse fails to occupy their God-ordained role: Ephesians 5:22 Wives, submit yourselves unto your own husbands, as unto the Lord.

[23] For the husband is the head of the wife, even as Christ is the head of the church: and he is the saviour of the body.

[24] Therefore as the church is subject unto Christ, so let the wives be to their own husbands in every thing.

[25] Husbands, love your wives, even as Christ also loved the church, and gave himself for it;

[26] That he might sanctify and cleanse it with the washing of water by the word,

[27] That he might present it to himself a glorious church, not having spot, or wrinkle, or any such thing; but that it should be holy and without blemish.

[28] So ought men to love their wives as their own bodies. He that loveth his wife loveth himself.

[29] For no man ever yet hated his own flesh; but nourisheth and cherisheth it, even as the Lord the church:

[30] For we are members of his body, of his flesh, and of his bones.

[31] For this cause shall a man leave his father and mother, and shall be joined unto his wife, and they two shall be one flesh.

[32] This is a great mystery: but I speak concerning Christ and the church.

[33] Nevertheless let every one of you in particular so love his wife even as himself; and the wife see that she reverences her husband.

This is an amazing Bible passage written for the family. The two essential elements we need to explore here are the functions of the spouse in the home; the husband must love and the wife must submit:

Husband, love your wife as Christ loves His church: This is one of the most frightening sentences in the Bible to me because if I am to love my wife according to God's standards, I must study the life of Jesus. This is why many husbands fail in their God-given purpose and make life difficult in the home. As a husband, you are not permitted to change your personality because your wife is not up to your standard. According to the Bible, Jesus died for us while we were still sinners; He did not compromise His character because we did not appreciate His death; He hung on and interceded for us until Christ was formed in us. I was recently on social media when a man stated that he began womanizing because his wife was unfaithful. This is not true; nothing should lead you to change your character against your wife since you are representing Christ in that home.

I charge you to keep your eyes fixed on Christ, and He will help you. If you do not hold to God, you will hold to the devil, you will misbehave and live your life the way you want. A man who does not represent Christ is the one who beats and abuses his wife in the house, a man who does not accept his position is the one who makes home tough for the wife. Allow Christ to be the Lord of your home, and you will see things work out for the best.

Wife, Submit to your husband: What this represents in the text is what we need to evaluate. The Bible says, "wife submit as unto the Lord." If you consider this, you will realize that what the scripture is driving out here is total submission. One issue that is damaging our marriage is that many wives constantly repeat that we are new generation Christians, with no male or female, thus submission is unnecessary. They claim to be equal with the man. May I say to you that no man wants to live with another man in the home. Man always wants to feel as if he is the leader in the home, and if he discovers that anyone is attempting to challenge his position, he will defend it with all his strength, and in doing so, many things will be affected, including the joy you once shared, the peace, the smile, and the intimacy. Before you know it, a glorious home will turn to a toxic home.

Dear Ma'am, I beg you in Jesus' name, don't live in your home as if you are the head, submit to him in all things. Don't claim to submit but your words are full of abuses, he may not take it. If you are both doing house chores together, let him know you appreciate it, and if you need him to assist you again, ask him with humility, I see God helping your home in Jesus' name.

Emotional abuse: We need to check this scripture: Ephesians 4:29 [29] Let no corrupt communication proceed out of your mouth, but that which is good to the use of edifying, that it may minister grace unto the hearers.

Whatever you are saying to your spouse is what he will become sooner or later. Many people have left their husband's house as a result of emotional abuse, because they couldn't cope anymore. The husband would complain about virtually everything; she doesn't know how to cook, she doesn't know how to communicate, she doesn't know how to entertain visitors. I understand that some women fall into this category, but that should not be the reason for you to emotionally abuse her.

On your wedding day, you were referred to as groom and bride for a reason. You will be the one to groom her until she becomes the kind of wife you want. Many brilliant sisters have lost their vision because the one man who should have appreciated them didn't. Even when strangers compliment her, it means nothing to her because her trusted man has killed her zeal, he has killed her passion.

I make sure I push my wife encouragingly to achieve things she thinks she can't. I became her first audience; I appreciate her before others do. I tell of how much I like her beauty daily. I am always positive about her, and as a result, she has soared and is always happy. If your wife is smiling outdoors but always moody in the home, you should be questioned. The best life you can live is couple's life; I've never regretted marrying, and I'm grateful to God that I did. I don't feel like I should appreciate my singlehood more since my marriage has exposed me to greatness, pleasure, and satisfaction.

Whatever it is, you can change it right now by going to your wife, or talking to your husband, apologizing for the emotional harm you have inflicted, and working on how to bring out the best in each other.

Physical abuse: This is becoming a daily issue around us. It is painful that the same man who professed love to you not long ago has now turned you into a punching bag without pity. I am still perplexed as to how a man can beat up his wife and go on with his life as if nothing happened. I am still puzzled as to how a man can feel happy to hit his wife in front of the children. I am still baffled as to how you brought that beautiful woman from her parent's house to be beaten. I realize that women may be abusive with their words, but it should not be the basis for your beating. Any man who beats his wife is the same as a lunatic on the street. If God can open his eyes to see the destruction he is wreaking on

his destiny, he will quickly repent. See the scripture: Ephesians 3:7

[7] Likewise, ye husbands, dwell with them according to knowledge, giving honour unto the wife, as unto the weaker vessel, and as being heirs together of the grace of life; that your prayers be not hindered.

The quality provided to women in this chapter is sufficient to protect them from any abuse. You are not authorized to maltreat her in any form. The Bible confirms that if you treat your wife against God's desire, your prayer will be unanswered. See another scripture against this:

Colossians 3: [19] Husbands, love your wives, and be not bitter against them.

Another version says "…and don't be harsh on them" It is so bad nowadays that some husbands would rather direct their rage at whatever occurred at work at their spouses; this is not acceptable; we cannot continue in this manner; God's purpose will not be fulfilled if one partner is unhappy at home.

The painful aspect is that those men who beat their wives do not realize they are missing out on a lot of life's fortunes. They believe they are all in all; they do not realize that they cannot be called husbands without wife. Your wife came to complement you; she came to add beauty to you. She left everything she had; you diverted her journey; you changed her appearance; she bears your name; she carries your pregnancy; she went into labour for you; some delivered through cesarean; she did all these just for you. Your children will be named after your name, not hers; beating should not be the reward for such a lady. It is preferable to repent now and seek God's favour.

Dear woman going through this, I want you to know that your husband is possessed by the devil; he may attend church, be a pastor, or hold a position; the devil has possession of him as long as he is abusing you. That is why, at first, he will apologise for beating you, saying he doesn't know what came over him, however, as time goes on, he will stop apologising because he has sold his soul to the devil. Such a man needs deliverance, the devil is using him to carry out his destabilising goal, and he cooperated with the devil. I pray that such men who are under the devil's control be delivered in Jesus' name.

Many waves of abuse may put marriage in jeopardy. We've covered a lot in this chapter, but allow me to mention one more point before I wrap up.

Financial abuse: In certain cultures, the wife is solely married to cook and stay in the house. She is not permitted to do anything else, and the husband denies her his income. This is not how it is ordained; whatever income both parties earn belongs to the family. Why will one party continue to enjoy the money while the other suffers for it? Why will you hide your money when you know how important the assignment is? don't go out and spend your salary alone, only to return home to find your family hungry. Don't eat good food before returning home, only to allow your family to eat what is available. Don't wear the best fabric while your family suffers in silence; instead, let them know that what you have is theirs. Be thoughtful about them!
See what the Bible says: 1Tim.5.8 - But if anyone does not provide for his own, and especially for those of his household, he has denied the faith and is worse than an unbeliever.
Some men are blessed, but, out of wickedness, they just choose to be selfish. They only care about themselves. This is not right according the scripture above.

Ask for forgiveness today and repent of your wrongdoing.

DIVORCE AND SEPARATION

Chapter Ten

We have seen a lot of theories on this subject, and I want to let you know that I am not going to speak different theory, instead, we will examine the text together to determine what God's thought is on this matter.

We will start by considering the teaching of Jesus, then we will check what Moses and the law says.

Matthew 19:3-9 **3** The Pharisees also came unto him, tempting him, and saying unto him, Is it lawful for a man to put away his wife for every cause?

4 And he answered and said unto them, Have ye not read, that he which made them at the beginning made them male and female,

5 And said, For this cause shall a man leave father and mother, and shall cleave to his wife: and they twain shall be one flesh?

6 Wherefore they are no more twain, but one flesh. What therefore God hath joined together, let not man put asunder.

7 They say unto him, Why did Moses then command to give a writing of divorcement, and to put her away?

8 He saith unto them, Moses because of the hardness of your hearts suffered you to put away your wives: but from the beginning it was not so.

⁹ And I say unto you, Whosoever shall put away his wife, except it be for fornication, and shall marry another, committeth adultery: and whoso marrieth her which is put away doth commit adultery.

We need to check critically some points here, the first point was the response of Moses, and the second point is "**Whosoever shall put away his wife, except it be for fornication**" the third point **"but from the beginning, it was not so."**

I will need to start from the last point mentioned above:
God's plan before the fall of man was for a husband to live only with his wife, which is why God created one man and one woman. God didn't give man an option, telling him that if their marriage doesn't work, he could marry another person. Man was created in God's image and there was no room for divorce. Everything began with man's fall when he was exposed through the fruit, as well as listening to the devil's dictate. See Jesus' response when they questioned Him why Moses had permitted it.

⁸ He saith unto them, Moses because of the hardness of your hearts...

One important point to note is that the law of Moses was instituted as a result of man's hardness of heart. Keep in mind what the Bible says in Genesis 6:5 And God saw that the wickedness of man was great in the earth, and that every imagination of the thoughts of his heart was only evil continually.

As man grew, so did sin; man couldn't hold on to marriage vow any longer, and the law of Moses came into effect, stating that if your spouse's heart was hard and he couldn't repent, don't die in silence, divorce him; however, Christ is saying that this was not God's plan. He opposes divorce, which is why Jesus came to restore us to God's original purpose for man to live in peace and love with the bride of his youth for the rest of his life. See the scripture about this: Ezekiel 11: [19] And I will give them one heart, and I will put a new spirit within you; and I will take the stony heart out of their flesh, and will give them an heart of flesh: [20] That they may walk in my statutes, and keep mine ordinances, and do them: and they shall be my people, and I will be their God.

No man with a hard heart can please God, and if such a man marries, he may make the home toxic for the spouse, which is why Christ came, to bring man back to God, to reclaim the heart of man that had been possessed by the devil and restore it to God. See Apostle Paul's prayer in the book of 1 Thessalonians 3: [11] Now God himself and our Father, and our Lord Jesus Christ, direct our way unto you. [12] And the Lord make you to increase and abound in love one toward another, and toward all men, even as we do toward you:

[13] To the end he may stablish your hearts unblameable in holiness before God, even our Father, at the coming of our Lord Jesus Christ with all his saints.

Jesus came to establish the heart of man blameless with God so that the heart of man can be broken for the word of God to germinate and expand, You will agree with me that our desire to receive the word differs because the outcome of the word is determined by how broken a man's heart is. No word of God can live in a stony heart, which is why attending church services can never determine if a man or woman is a suitable husband or wife. It is two people that have been broken, transformed and regenerated, but if otherwise, it takes the grace of God for such home to stand.

Here, we will check one word mentioned by Christ "And I say unto you, Whosoever shall put away his wife, **except it be for fornication**," We will take a deep study on this as we trust God to give us understanding. Why did Jesus put a clause here? That you can decide to put away your spouse on the altar of fornication?

This is a mystery that must be unfolded. When a husband and wife marry, they become one through covenant, just as we become one with Christ through His blood. As long as a man abides in Christ, he is bound by His blood, but he has the option to walk away. Walking out of the covenant with Christ means he is no longer bound to Christ and may do anything he wants. Similarly, sleeping with another man or woman in marriage is a violation of the divine covenant of marriage because the zeal that joined them together has been compromised and the blood contaminated. At this point, two things can happen: The first is that the other spouse who is standing can stand as Christ did for mankind and restore the fallen partner into the covenant. This is what Adam should have done when Eve died. Adam was still alive, and the Spirit of God was still in him; he could have stood in the gap and brought Eve back to life, instead he died with her. The second thing is that he can choose not to marry again, but because Christ is our priority, we must do everything we can to forgive our spouse. Please keep in mind that forgiveness does not imply that you will not take appropriate action in a case where a temporary separation is required if the situation is life-threatening. We will discuss this further as we progress through this chapter. Apostle Paul gave us a clear explanation on this, please let us see it:

1Corinthinas 7:10-15 And unto the married I command, yet not I, but the Lord, Let not the wife depart from her husband:

[11] But and if she depart, let her remain unmarried or be reconciled to her husband: gyand let not the husband put away his wife.

[12] But to the rest speak I, not the Lord: If any brother hath a wife that believeth not, and she be pleased to dwell with him, let him not put her away.

[13] And the woman which hath an husband that believeth not, and if he be pleased to dwell with her, let her not leave him.

[14] For the unbelieving husband is sanctified by the wife, and the unbelieving wife is sanctified by the husband: else were your children unclean; but now are they holy.

[15] But if the unbelieving depart, let him depart. A brother or a sister is not **under bondage in such cases**: but God hath called us to peace.

Let us check out two things that Apostle Paul said: he spoke the mind of God and talked as an Apostle of God.

God underlines the value of marriage in divine plan in verses ten and eleven, stating that a wife must not leave her husband and vice - versa, but if he does, he must remain unmarried. This suggests that the situation may call for it, and they've tried and failed to make it work. Don't forget what I said about the hardness of heart; perhaps the situation warrants letting go, and this decision must be reached in consultation with the elders of your local church; it must have been a reason totally against the scripture that the other party Is not ready to change.

The second he spoke about is the union between a believer and an unbeliever. I want you to know that this is a critical issue. Apostle Paul said if you have an unbelieving husband or wife you are free to live with them:

[14] For the unbelieving husband is sanctified by the wife, and the unbelieving wife is sanctified by the husband. By staying with an unbeliever, you will be able to transform him by Christ that you have. See verse 15 again: [15] But if the unbelieving depart, let him depart.

A brother or a sister is not **under bondage in such cases**: but God hath called us to peace. Apostle Paul established that if the unbelieving depart, please note it, he is speaking to the unbeliever, who has decided to leave the marriage for one reason or another and is not willing to abide by the marriage covenant, and you have tried to persuade him not to leave, but he has made up his mind. You are not under any yoke, according to the Bible, if you perceive a Christian willing to marry you in the future. The reason is that light and light can only live together, darkness and light can never be covenanted together, something will separate them at some point.

When it comes to divorce and separation, I believe that some circumstances may warrant it, but let the leadership of your church decide. That is why you must be rooted and grounded in a local church, and when you can no longer bear the pain, open up to your local church, or your family third party, as explained in this book.

Matthew 18: [15] Moreover if thy brother shall trespass against thee, go and tell him his fault between thee and him alone: if he shall hear thee, thou hast gained thy brother.

[16] But if he will not hear thee, then take with thee one or two more, that in the mouth of two or three witnesses every word may be established.

[17] And if he shall neglect to hear them, tell it unto the church: but if he neglect to hear the church, let him be unto thee as an heathen man and a publican.

All of these stages must be put in place before considering separation and divorce. After all of the appropriate procedures have been taken and the other person has refused to change and continues to live in a way that negatively affects the other's life, the church must order separation for a while continuing to pray for the second party, but if he refuses to obey God's direction and continues in his wickedness, the Bible calls him a dead man, and the covenant between him and the other party is broken.
The last sentence of Apostle Paul in that verse is a good point to end this chapter with, he said "but God hath called us to peace" In other words, God is not pleased with divorce; he wants the home to be a place of peace and harmony, which is exactly what Christ came to achieve for us. However, if the man continues to have a hard heart and refuses to change, the necessary steps must be taken to ensure that the partner's life is not cut short.

CONCLUSION

Chapter Eleven

I'm excited to have reached the conclusion of this book. In the process of writing, I've learned and unlearned. I have implemented what I've learned here in my home and seen incredible results. I hope God will use this book to transform and change your home in Jesus' name.

I'd like to encourage you to set aside time to pray on many of the issues raised in this book. Don't just read it and walk away; instead, try to work on yourself, do a personal evaluation; pick up a pen and paper, and itemise the areas you believe your spouse is complaining about. Be deliberate in your transformation, It might be fast or slow, but make sure you are not on the same level. The devil may convince you that you won't be able to reclaim your home; remind him that your home belongs to Jesus and that He will fight your battle in Jesus' name.

Never lose hope in your spouse; you may have done your best, but it was not God's best. Check the weapon you're using, seek God for a solution, stay positive, don't talk too much, turn your grumbling to prayer and let the heavens hear you

The worst mistake you can do is to repay evil with evil. Don't start being unfaithful because he is unfaithful, instead, be true to your marital vow and trust God to see you through.

Let us pray;
Jesus, you are the owner of this home, you brought them together for a purpose, I declare all-round peace over this home in Jesus' name, I speak against the storm from the devil that gives you no rest and I ask that the hand of the Lord fight your battle in Jesus name. Amen.

ABOUT THE AUTHOR

Yemi Adebanjo

Yemi Adebanjo is is a servant of God and a marriage and single counselor who has been given the assignment of raising Kingdom men with relevance. He was sent with the specific goal of impacting men with godliness in order to impact the world. As a result, He desired to see people burning for Christ and having amazing marriage everywhere and in every place with the mindset of taking possession for Christ, to raise the banner of righteousness and godliness, to see men do things right, and to see people willingly submit to God.

He is a visioner of Christian Single Summit, and is a Pastor in charge of Living Truth Christian Centre Mararaba, Abuja. He is blessed with beautiful wifc and two amazing children

In 2009, through God's grace, he founded the Excellent Power of God Ministry. The Lord has utilized this interdenominational ministry to empower people for himself and to advance his kingdom. He is the Pastor in charge of Living Truth Christian Center in Abuja Nigeria. he is blessed with a beautiful wife Joy Adebanjo and two amazing children.

You can reach him for your feedback,discussion and question through

Yemiadebanj24@gmail.com or his whatsapp number on +2348062393905